Opus 38

Heinz Tesar
Sammlung Essl, Klosterneuburg

**Text
Gottfried Knapp**

**Photographien / Photographs
Christian Richters**

Edition Axel Menges

Herausgeber/Editor: Axel Menges

© 2000 Edition Axel Menges, Stuttgart/London
ISBN 3-930698-40-4

Alle Rechte vorbehalten, besonders die der Übersetzung in andere Sprachen.
All rights reserved, especially those of translation into other languages.

Reproduktionen/Reproductions: Bild & Text Joachim Baun, Fellbach
Druck/Printing: Rösler Druck GmbH, Schorndorf
Bindearbeiten/Binding: Verlagsbuchbinderei Karl Dieringer, Gerlingen

Übersetzung ins Englische/Translation into English: Michael Robinson
Design: Axel Menges

Inhalt

6   Gottfried Knapp: Raumfiguren für die Kunst – Heinz Tesars Museumsbau für die Sammlung Essl in Klosterneuburg

16 Pläne
    Perspektive der Gesamtsituation 16 – Lageplan 17 – Grundrisse 18 – Schnitte und Aufrisse 20 – Perspektiven 22

24 Bildteil
    Gesamtansichten 24 – Detailansichten 32 – Haupttreppenhaus 38 – Innenhof 40 – Laternen auf dem Galerietrakt 41 – Galerietrakt 42 – Ausstellungstrakt 48 – Depot 56 – Abschied 58

60 Daten

Contents

7   Gottfried Knapp: Spatial figures for art – Heinz Tesar's museum building for the Essl Collection in Klosterneuburg

16 Pläne
    Perspective view of the general situation 16 – Site plan 17 – Floor plans 18 – Sections and elevations 20 – Perspective views 22

24 Pictorial section
    General views 24 – Detailed views 32 – Main staircase 38 – Courtyard 40 – Lanterns on the gallery wing 41 – Gallery wing 42 – Exhibition wing 48 – Storage area 56 – Final view 58

60 Dates

Gottfried Knapp
Raumfiguren für die Kunst – Heinz Tesars Museumsbau für die Sammlung Essl in Klosterneuburg

Wer sich ohne nähere Kenntnis des Ortes auf der unscheinbaren Zubringerstraße dem hoch geschlossenen, langgezogenen Architekturgebilde nähert oder es per Zufall vom vorbeifahrenden Zug aus entdeckt, wird dessen Zweck wohl schwerlich erraten. Mit den bekannten Grundtypen heutigen Bauens, mit Wohn-, Industrie-, Verwaltungs- oder Sakralbauten hat diese Rätselarchitektur kaum etwas gemein. Sie muß eher ungewöhnlichen Aufgaben dienen. Und tatsächlich umschließt das Gebäude etwas, was man hier, im chaotisch verbauten Gewerbegebiet zwischen Bahndamm und Donauauen, am wenigsten erwartet: ein Museum zeitgenössischer Kunst, ein Kulturforum, wie es in dieser Form in Europa bisher nicht existiert hat. Das auffällige Gebäude beherbergt die wohl umfassendste Privatsammlung neuerer Kunst in Österreich. Es wird in jeder Hinsicht privat, also ohne öffentliche Zuschüsse betrieben; dennoch ist es mit allem ausgestattet, was zu einem repräsentativen Museum gehört: mit Depots, Restaurierungswerkstätten, einer eigenen Museumsmannschaft und auch dem nötigen Betriebskapital.

Agnes und Karlheinz Essl haben als junge Leute in Amerika das generös-mäzenatische Wirken der Oberschicht kennengelernt und erste Erfahrungen mit den bildenden Künsten, mit dem amerikanischen Galeriensystem, mit Kunstfreunden und Künstlern gemacht. Nach ihrer Rückkehr aus den USA und nach der Heirat trat Karlheinz Essl in das Unternehmen seines Schwiegervaters Schömer in Klosterneuburg ein und begann jene Kette von Heimwerkermärkten mit dem Namen »bauMax« aufzubauen, die heute in Österreich und Osteuropa führend ist.

Das Sammeln von Kunst wurde zur zweiten Profession der Eheleute Essl. Innerhalb von 30 Jahren haben sie eine Sammlung aufgebaut, die zumindest auf dem Gebiet der neueren österreichischen Kunst ohne Konkurrenz ist. Und von Anfang an war es ihnen eine Selbstverständlichkeit, die wachsenden Schätze in Katalogen zu publizieren und der Öffentlichkeit in Ausstellungen zugänglich zu machen. So sind bedeutende Teile der Sammlung im Auftrag des österreichischen Ministeriums für Auswärtige Angelegenheiten als kulturelle Botschafter um die ganze Welt gereist.

Im Jahr 1990 machten die Essls dann dem österreichischen Staat das Angebot, ihre Sammlung in das geplante Museumsquartier auf dem Gelände der ehemaligen Hofstallungen in Wien zu überführen. Ihre Idee war, hierfür den von den Museumsarchitekten vorgeschlagenen, aber in der Öffentlichkeit umstrittenen »Bücherturm« als Galeriegebäude zu nutzen und so ein wesentliches Element des Gesamtplans für das kulturelle Großunternehmen des Landes zu retten. Doch die von der Presse aufgehetzten Gegner des kühnen Unternehmens hatten sich in der Öffentlichkeit bereits darauf festgelegt, den Turm nicht zu bauen. Es war den Politikern offensichtlich nicht bewußt, daß sie mit ihrer Ablehnung eine Sammlung von Weltrang, die den Bilderbestand der teuer erworbenen Sammlung Leopold auf dem gleichen Niveau bis in die Gegenwart verlängert hätte, aus Wien vertrieben. Für die Essls war die Ablehnung durch den Staat der Anlaß, an ein eigenes Ausstellungshaus und an ein zentrales Bilderdepot in der eigenen Stadt zu denken und so der mäzenatischen Arbeit in Klosterneuburg eine neue Dimension zu geben.

Schon seit 1987, seit der Eröffnung ihres neuen Verwaltungszentrums, des Schömer-Hauses in Klosterneuburg, zeigten die Essls in der eigens dafür konzipierten zentralen Halle Teile der Sammlung; sie organisierten ambitionierte Einzelpräsentationen für Maler ihrer Wahl wie Arnulf Rainer, luden Aktionskünstler wie Hermann Nitsch zu höchst spektakulären Aktionen ein und öffneten das Haus für die Neue Musik: Unter der Leitung ihres Sohnes, des Komponisten Karlheinz Essl junior, wurden höchst anspruchsvolle internationale Avantgardekonzerte veranstaltet, ja sogar Kompositionsaufträge vergeben.

Den einzigartigen Rahmen für all diese vielfältigen künstlerischen Aktivitäten – das Schömer-Haus – hatte Heinz Tesar entworfen. Und da der Bau viel gelobt wurde, lag es nahe, daß sich die Mäzene auch bei ihren anderen Stiftungswerken wieder mit dem eigenwilligen Wiener Künstler-Architekten zusammentaten, der beim Schömer-Haus so viel raumästhetisches Gefühl, so viel Bewußtsein für die Belange der Künste gezeigt hatte. So kam es zu der gloriosen Dreiheit von Kult- und Kulturbauten in jener Stadt bei Wien, die bis dahin nur ihres grandiosen Augustiner-Chorherrenstiftes und der darin bewahrten mittelalterlichen Kunstschätze wegen im Bewußtsein der kunstinteressierten Weltöffentlichkeit existiert hatte.

Für die gläubigen Protestanten Agnes und Karlheinz Essl – auch das haben sie in den USA studieren können – war der erworbene Besitz immer auch eine Verpflichtung gegenüber der Öffentlichkeit. In einem Gespräch hat Karlheinz Essl einmal gesagt: »Besitz bedeutet Verantwortung. Das kommt aus meiner protestantischen Überzeugung heraus. Ein Teil von dem, was wir erwirtschaften konnten, soll wieder einer breiteren Öffentlichkeit zugute kommen.«

Wie das geht, haben die Essls zunächst mit dem Kulturprogramm im Schömer-Haus vorgeführt. In den neunziger Jahren haben sie dann weitere kräftige Zeichen gesetzt: Sie haben den Bau einer neuen evangelischen Kirche in Klosterneuburg ermöglicht und ihren eigenen Kunstbesitz in eine Stiftung überführt, die den ständig wachsenden Bestand bewahren und in einem eigenen Ausstellungshaus der Welt vermitteln sollte. Und da sie die Architektur für diese beiden neuen Projekte wieder Heinz Tesar anvertrauten, rundete sich die Arbeit des Architekten in Klosterneuburg zu einem höchst anspruchsvollen Gesamtkomplex, den man nur als Glücksfall für die Architektur empfinden kann.

Bevor wir uns etwas eingehender mit dem Haus der Sammlung Essl beschäftigen, wollen wir zunächst kurz die beiden mit diesem spannungsvoll kommunizierenden und kontrastierenden Vorläuferbauten in Klosterneuburg betrachten.

Das Schömer-Haus, in dem die Hauptverwaltung des »bauMax« sitzt, gibt sich nach außen als Verwaltungsbau zu erkennen, nimmt also die temporäre Zusatzfunktion als Kulturforum ganz ins Innere zurück. Der viergeschossige, symmetrisch gegliederte Kubus auf rechteckigem Grundriß ist in den einzelnen Stockwerken mit minimalen Mitteln – mit raffinierten Kurvierungen – geschickt differenziert. So tut sich über dem Haupteingang eine dreigeschossige Nische mit kurvierter Rückwand auf. Auf der Rückseite springt das Kasino im Erdgeschoß wie ein Mittelrisalit mit einer kon-

Gottfried Knapp
Spatial figures for art – Heinz Tessar's museum building for the Essl Collection in Klosterneuburg

Anyone approaching this long, tall, closed architectural structure on the unassuming access road or discovering it by chance from a passing train will have difficulty in working out what it is for. This mysterious architecture has scarcely anything in common with modern building's familiar basic types for housing, offices or churches. It must be for some unusual purpose. And indeed the building does contain something that is most unexpected here, in the chaotically ill-built commercial area between the railway line and the meadows by the Danube: it is a museum of contemporary art, a cultural forum that has so far not existed in this form in Europe. This striking building contains what is probably the most comprehensive collection of recent art in Austria. It is private in every respect, that is to say it is run without any public subsidy; and yet it has everything that one associates with a prestigious museum: storage space, restoration workshops, its own museum team and also the necessary working capital.

Agnes and Karlheinz Essl became familiar with the generosity with which upper-class Americans give patronage to the arts while spending time there as young people, and gained their first experience of fine art, the American gallery system, art-lovers and artists. After coming home from the United States and getting married, Karheinz Essl joined his father-in-law Schomer's business in Klosterneuburg and start to build up the chain of do-it-yourself stores called »bauMax«, which is now a market leader in Austria and Eastern Europe.

Collecting art became a second profession for the Essls. They have built up a collection over thirty years that is unequalled, at least in the field of recent Austrian art. And from the outset they took it for granted that they should publish their accumulated treasures in catalogues and make them accessible to the public in exhibitions. Thus significant parts of the collection have travelled the world as cultural ambassadors on behalf of the Austrian Ministry of Foreign Affairs.

In 1990 the Essls suggested to the Austrian state that they would be prepared to place their collection in the planned museum quarter on the site of the former court stables in Vienna. Their idea was to use the »Book Tower«, which had been proposed by the architects but had proved controversial with the public, as a gallery and thus rescue a fundamental element of the whole plan for the country's major cultural enterprise. But the opponents of this bold enterprise, who had been stirred up by the press, had already brought about a public decision that the tower should not be built. The politicians were obviously not aware that by this act of rejection they had driven a world-class collection out of Vienna. It would have complemented the Leopold Collection, which had been acquired at considerable expense, by providing contemporary art on the same level. For the Essls, rejection by the state made them think of an exhibition building of their own and a central repository for pictures in their home town, thus giving a new dimension to patronage of the arts in Klosterneuburg.

Ever since 1987, when their new headquarters, the Schömer-Haus in Klosterneuburg opened, the Essls had been showing part of the collection in the central hall, which was specially conceived for this purpose; they organized ambitious one-man shows for painters of their choice like Arnulf Rainer, invited action artists like Hermann Nitsch to create spectacular actions and opened up the building for new music: high-calibre international avant-garde concerts were put on under the direction of their son, the composer Karlheinz Essl junior, and some new music was even commissioned.

Heinz Tesar had designed the Schömer-Haus, which provided a unique frame for all these various cultural activities. And as the building had been much praised, it made sense for the patrons to team up with this unconventional Viennese artist-architect again, as he had shown so much sensitivity to space and aesthetics and so much awareness of the needs of art in the Schömer-Haus. And so that town near Vienna, which had hitherto been in the consciousness of the world public only for its wonderful Augustinian Chorherrenstift, and the medieval art treasures housed in it, now has a glorious trinity of ecclesiastical and secular buildings as well.

Agnes and Karlheinz Essl, who are practising Protestants, always saw the possessions they had acquired as giving them a commitment to the public – something else they were able to study in the USA. Karlheinz Essl once said in an interview: »Possessions mean responsibility. This comes from my Protestant convictions. Part of everything we have been able to obtain by careful management should benefit a wider public again.«

The Essls showed how this worked first of all with the cultural programme in the Schömer-Haus. They then set another powerful example in the nineties: they made it possible to build a new Protestant church in Klosterneuburg and placed their own art collection in a trust that was to look after the steadily growing body of work and display it to the world in a custom-built exhibition building. And as they once more put Heinz Tesar in charge of the architecture for these two new projects, the architect's work in Klosterneuburg became a highly prestigious complete project that can only be seen as a happy chance for architecture.

Before we look at the building for the Essl Collection in more detail, we would first like to look at the two earlier buildings in Klosterneuburg, which communicate and contrast with this excitingly.

The Schömer-Haus, which contains the headquarters of »bauMax«, looks like an office building from the outside, in other words it hides its temporary additional function as a cultural forum well away inside itself. The four-storey, symmetrically articulated cube on a square ground plan is skilfully broken down into individual floors using a minimum of resources – sophisticated curves. Thus there is a three-storey niche with a curved rear wall above the main entrance. On the rear side, the canteen leaps forward on the ground floor like a central projection with a concave curve in its façade, in the two storeys above this the outer wall curves outwards in a convex counter-movement, and on the fourth floor the four corners of the building are omitted so that four roof terraces with curved walls open up.

The outside walls follow various segment arcs, sometimes convex and sometimes concave, and there is a response to this in the interior from a huge, transverse-oval central hall rising through all four storeys, with galleries running round it, showing parts of the art collection at all times. This oval arena of the arts with

1. Heinz Tesar, Schömer-Haus, Klosterneuburg.
(Photo: Margeritha Spiluttini.)
2. Heinz Tesar, evangelische Kirche in Klosterneuburg.
(Photo: Mischa Erben.)
3. Heinz Tesar, Sammlung Essl, Klosterneuburg.
(Photo: Christian Richters.)

1. Heinz Tesar, Schömer-Haus, Klosterneuburg.
(Photo: Margeritha Spiluttini.)
2. Heinz Tesar, Protestant church in Klosterneuburg.
(Photo: Mischa Erben.)
3. Heinz Tesar, Sammlung Essl, Klosterneuburg.
(Photo: Christian Richters.)

kav gekurvten Front nach vorn, in den beiden Geschossen darüber wölbt sich die Außenwand in einer Gegenbewegung konvex nach außen, und im vierten Stock sind die vier Ecken des Gebäudes so ausgespart, daß sich dort vier Dachterrassen mit gekurvten Wänden auftun.

Den diversen Segmentbögen, denen die Außenwände mal konvex, mal konkav folgen, antwortet im Inneren eine durch alle Geschosse reichende riesige querovale Mittelhalle mit umlaufenden Galerien, an deren Wänden ständig Teile der Kunstsammlung ausgestellt sind. Diese ovale Arena der Künste wirkt mit ihren vier Rundumgalerien wie der moderne Nachbau eines Renaissance-Theaters – und wie in dieser Urform eines Zuschauerraums funktioniert auch die Akustik in der Halle so selbstverständlich, daß Konzerte jeder Größenordnung denkbar sind.

Überspannt wird das Oval, in dem schon ein kleines Stück Avantgarde-Geschichte geschrieben wurde, von einer flachen Decke, über der eine große runde Laterne zum Tageslicht emporragt und ein Kranz von kleinen runden Lichtkuppeln zusätzlich Oberlicht nach unten transportiert. Beherrschendes plastisches Element im Raum ist das in der Mittelachse mächtig in den Raum vorspringende zweiläufig-symmetrische Treppengehäuse, das mit seinen »Treillagen« – dem Lineament seiner senkrecht verlaufenden Metallstangen – und mit der oben aufsitzenden plastischen Figur den skulpturalen Anspruch des Architekten kräftig unterstreicht und daran erinnert, daß Tesar ja selber einmal bildnerisch tätig war, bevor er als Architekt bekannt wurde.

Im Schömer-Haus kommen sich also eine ausgeprägte Rationalität und eine fast obsessive Lust am eigensinnig geformten Detail, an bestimmten, immer wiederkehrenden Formen, höchst kreativ ins Gehege. Eine Folge von Fluren, die im Grundriß zusammen ein Rechteck bilden, verbindet im Inneren alle Arbeitsräume miteinander. In den Restflächen zwischen den

its four galleries running the full way round it seems like a modern copy of a Renaissance theatre, and as in this prototype of an auditorium the acoustics of the hall can be taken absolutely for granted, so that concerts of any size can function perfectly.

The oval, in which a little bit of avant-garde history has already been written, is spanned by a flat ceiling above which a large round lantern towers up to the daylight, and a garland of small round light-domes admit additional daylight from above. The dominant three-dimensional element in the space is the housing for the double-flighted, symmetrical staircase, which thrusts powerfully into the space on the central axis. Its »trelliswork« – the lines of its vertical metal rods – and the three-dimensional figure placed at the top powerfully underline the architect's sculptural aspirations and remind us that Tesar did indeed work in this field before he became known as an architect.

And so in the Schömer-Haus a marked sense of rationality and an almost obsessive delight in unconventionally formed detail, in certain shapes that constantly recur, are brought very creatively into play. A sequence of corridors, which together form a rectangle in the ground plan, links all the working rooms in the interior with each other. The lifts and toilets are accommodated in the spaces left between the surrounding corridors and the large, inscribed oval space. Thus the building is perfectly symmetrical in ground plan and elevation.

umlaufenden Fluren und dem einbeschriebenen großen Raumoval sind die Lifte und die Toiletten untergebracht. Im Grund- und Aufriß bietet sich das Haus also perfekt symmetrisch dar. Doch eine Fülle von weichen, gerundeten Formen, von Kreisen, Kreissegmenten und ihren Längungen ins Ovale, schneidet in die strenge Rechteckordnung ein, wölbt sich aus ihr heraus oder ist, wie in dem fischbauchförmigen Vordach über dem Windfang des Haupteingangs, den Geraden vorgelagert. Auch das Ineinander von Kreis und Oval, wie es an der Decke der zentralen Halle zelebriert wird, oder die gekurvten Zipfel, in die das Vordach an der Chefecke oder die Muster im Steinboden der Halle auslaufen, gehören zum persönlichen Formenvokabular Tesars, das in all seinen Bauten in individuellen Variationen zum Einsatz kommt.

Die evangelische Kirche in Klosterneuburg ist sogar ganz aus Rundformen entwickelt. Ein Oval umgibt den Gemeinderaum; aus ihm treten die Wände an der Schmal- und an der Breitseite je einmal in sanfter Weitung ein Stück weit heraus, so als würden sie zu einer Spirale ansetzen. Sie öffnen die Außenwand so, daß durch den Schlitz an der Schmalseite Licht in den gerundeten Altarraum fällt. Die andere, die breitere Weitung öffnet sich zum Kirchenvorplatz hin; sie dient als Eingang und als Vorraum für die Besucher.

In das Oval des Innenraums ist über dem Eingang eine kreisförmige Orgelempore als skulpturales Element eingefügt. Eine flache Längstonne wölbt sich als Decke über dem eiförmigen Raum; sie ist von 25 runden Lichtkuppeln durchbrochen. Ein originelles Muster von Rechtecköffnungen in der gekurvten Südwand und rundum unter dem Gewölbeansatz bringt zusätzlich Licht herein. Der magisch geschlossene Kultraum bekommt also durch das Neben- und Ineinander verschiedener Rundformen und durch das hochindividuelle System der unterschiedlichen Lichtöffnungen seinen eigenwilligen Charakter.

Auch der dritte Bau, den Tesar im Auftrag der Familie Essl in Klosterneuburg errichtet hat, ist ein Solitär, auch er baut sich als geschlossene, plastisch differenzierte Einheit auf dem Grundstück auf. Das Haus für die Kunstsammlung Essl liegt ungefähr auf halber Strecke zwischen den kulturellen Fixpunkten des Ortes, dem Schömer-Haus und dem kuppelgekrönten barocken Prachtbau des Chorherrenstifts. Es bildet im Grundriß ein rechtwinkliges Dreieck, das mit seiner Hypotenuse parallel zur Bahntrasse verläuft und mit dem spitzen Winkel in Richtung Stift weist.

Hinter der kürzesten Seite, der nach Süden gerichteten, liegt der Eingangstrakt. Er enthält hinter der mit Fensterbändern gegliederten Fassade alle nicht unmittelbar für die Aufbewahrung und Präsentation der Kunstwerke bestimmten Funktionen: im Erdgeschoß die Eingangshalle für die Besucher mit Kasse und Garderobe sowie die Werkstätten und die Haustechnik; im ersten Zwischengeschoß Büros und eine Einliegerwohnung; im ersten Obergeschoß, dem Hauptausstellungsgeschoß, die durch zwei Stockwerke hinaufreichende Bibliothek; im zweiten Zwischengeschoß das ebenfalls zwei Stockwerke hohe Tonstudio für Karlheinz Essl junior; im zweiten Obergeschoß, dem Geschoß des Großen Saals, die Verwaltungsräume der Stiftung Essl und im turmartigen Aufbau an der westlichen Ecke schließlich ein Studio für Agnes Essl.

Der Aufzugsturm für diese fünf Geschosse ist als eigener Baukörper so vor die Fassade gestellt, daß schmale Lichtschlitze – wir werden ihnen noch öfter begegnen – zwischen Lift und Außenwand emporlaufen. Über eine leicht ansteigende Rampe betreten die Besucher das Erdgeschoß, das wegen des möglichen Donauhochwassers um einen Meter angehoben wurde. Aus der schlichten Kassen- und Garderobenhalle führt der Weg über die höchst reizvoll vor die senkrechten Lichtschlitze der Außenwand modellierte dreiläufige Treppe in das eigentliche Galeriegeschoß hinauf. Dort verlassen sie den Eingangstrakt und begeben sich in einen der beiden langgestreckten, nach Norden aufeinander zulaufenden Museumstrakte, die den begrünten Hof auf recht gegensätzliche Weise flankieren.

Was der Museumsbau in Klosterneuburg unter der hochgehobenen Plattform der Galerieräume birgt, kann alle staatlichen oder kommunalen Museen neidisch machen. In dem hohen, im Grundriß dreieckigen fensterlosen Sockel sind Depoträume von geradezu verschwenderischen Ausmaßen und vorbildlicher Funktionalität untergebracht. Kunsttransporter können auf der Ostseite so tief in das Depot hineinfahren, daß sie bei geschlossenen Toren über die Laderampen stufenlos entladen werden können. Im Depot hat Tesar eine zentrale Transportstraße mit seitlichen Aufbewahrungsräumen angelegt. Jede dieser Hallen enthält rechts und links eine dichte Folge querliegender beweglicher Bilderwände, die in den breiten Mittelflur herausgezogen werden können. Das Depot ist streng auf dem rechten Winkel aufgebaut, was bei dem dreieckigen Grundriß des Außenbaus zwangsläufig zu Konflikten führt. Tesar gleicht den kalkulierten Widerspruch dadurch aus, daß er im Depotgeschoß die Hypotenuse, die schräg verlaufende westliche Wand dreimal einknickt, also der inneren Rechteckordnung anpaßt, was außen als reizvolle formale Bereicherung empfunden wird und der zur Bahn gerichteten Fassade einen maschinenhaften Rhythmus, ja ein spürbares Tempo verleiht. Im Museumsgeschoß darüber läßt Tesar die Außenmauer ohne Unterbrechung durchlaufen; sie folgt also dort exakt der Hypotenuse des rechtwinkligen Grundrißdreiecks. Doch da die hier hintereinander geschalteten Galerieräume wie die Depoträume darunter an der Rechteckordnung der Katheten orientiert sind, gibt es in den sechs einander folgenden Galerieräumen zwangsläufig jeweils eine Wand – die Außenwand –, die schräg verläuft. Die Räume sind daher im Grundriß trapezförmig und schieben sich mit ihren rechteckigen Kopfseiten unterschiedlich weit in den Hof vor, so daß sich dort eine eigentümliche Staffelung ergibt.

Diesen Teil des Museumstraktes hat Tesar als Galerie, als eine Abfolge klassischer Oberlichträume ausgebaut. Und da er die Lichtöffnungen in den Decken genau der Raumform anpaßt, haben auch die aufgesetzten Laternen trapezförmige Grundrisse.

Bei der Belichtung variiert Tesar das von Leo von Klenze für die Alte Pinakothek in München entwickelte und bis heute kaum jemals übertroffene Oberlichtsystem auf recht suggestive Weise. Die hohen mächtigen Laternen, die wie Gewächshäuser auf dem Galerietrakt stehen, sind nach oben geschlossen. Sie nehmen durch ihre vier gläsernen Wände das Tageslicht auf. Jalousien auf der Außenseite und bewegliche Stoffvorhänge auf der Innenseite sorgen dafür, daß Sonnenstrahlen nicht direkt ins Innere dringen können. Das Licht wird also schon in der Laterne diffundiert und fällt als gleichmäßige, aber intensive Helligkeit in die Räume hinunter. Und da die Wände an ihren oberen Enden

But an abundance of soft, rounded forms, of circles, segments of circles and their elongations into ovals cut into the strict, square order, come curving out of it or are placed in front of straight lines, as in the fish-bellied canopy above the porch of the main entrance. Also linked circles and ovals, as celebrated in the roof of the central hall, or the curved tips into which the canopy on the management corner or the patterns on the stone floor of the hall run out are part of Tesar's personal formal vocabulary, which is used in individual variations in all his buildings.

The Protestant church in Klosterneuburg is in fact developed entirely from rounded forms. An oval surrounds the area for the congregation; from it the walls on the narrow and broad sides are each shifted outwards in a gentle widening movement that looks as though they are starting to form a spiral. They open up the outer wall in such a way that the slit on the narrow side admits light in the rounded chancel. The other, wider extension opens on to the square in front of the church; it serves as an entrance and an anteroom for visitors.

A circular organ-gallery is fitted into the oval of the interior as a sculptural element above the entrance. A shallow longitudinal barrel curves across the ovoid space to form the ceiling; it is pierced by 25 round light-domes. An unusual pattern of rectangular openings in the curved south wall and all the way around under the level at which the ceiling starts to rise provides additional light. The magically closed devotional room thus derives its unconventional character from the juxtaposition and interlinking of various curved forms and also from the highly individual system of different openings to provide light.

The third building that Tesar has built for the Essl family in Klosterneuburg is also a solitaire, and it too rises from its site as a closed, three-dimensionally differentiated unit. The building for the Essl Collection is roughly half-way between the town's fixed cultural points, the Schömer-Haus and the magnificent domed, Baroque building of the Chorherrenstift. Its ground plan is a right-angled triangle, with its hypotenuse parallel with the railway line and the acute angle pointing in the direction of the Chorherrenstift.

The entrance section is behind the shortest façade, which faces south. Behind the façade, which is articulated with continuous windows, it contains all the functions not directly concerned with storing and presenting the works of art: on the ground floor is the entrance hall for visitors with box office and cloakroom, and also the workshop and technical equipment; on the first mezzanine floor are offices and a flat; on the first floor, the main exhibition floor, is the library, which rises through two storeys; on the second mezzanine floor is the sound studio for Karlheinz Essl junior, which is also two storeys high; and finally on the second floor, which accommodates the Great Hall, the offices for the Essl Foundation and finally a studio for Agnes Essl in the tower-like structure on the west corner.

The lift tower for these floors is a building in its own right placed in front of the façade in such a way that narrow lighting slits – and we are going to come across these with increasing frequency – run up between the lift and the outside wall. Visitors come into the ground floor, which is raised by a metre because of possible flooding from the Danube, via a shallow ramp. The way out of the modest hall with box office and cloakroom leads via the three flights of stairs, charmingly placed in front of the vertical light slits in the outside wall, into the actual exhibition floor. There they leave the entrance section and move into one of the two long museum sections, running towards each other in a northerly direction, and flanking the planted courtyard in quite contrasting ways.

Any national or municipal museum would be envious of what the museum in Klosterneuburg has hidden away under the raised platform of the galleries. The tall, windowless base storey, triangular in ground plan, contains storerooms on an almost extravagant scale, that function in a model fashion. Art transporters can drive so deep into the store on the east side that they can be unloaded continuously via the loading ramps, with the main doors closed. Tesar has provided a central transport route with storerooms at the side in the store. To the right and left of each of these halls is a dense sequence of transverse walls for pictures, which can be pulled out into the broad central hall. The store is built rigorously on the right angle, which inevitably leads to conflicts, given the triangular ground plan of the outside building. Tesar balances out this calculated contradiction by introducing three bends into the hypotenuse, the west wall, which runs diagonally, on the store floor, in other words adapts it to the interior square order, which is seen as an attractive formal enrichment on the outside and gives the façade facing the railway a mechanical rhythm, indeed a detectable tempo. On the museum floor above this Tesar causes the external wall to run through without interruption; thus here it follows the hypotenuse of the right-angled triangle of the ground plan precisely. But as the gallery rooms, which are placed one behind the other here, like the storerooms below them, are oriented to the right-angled order of the legs of the triangle, in each of the six galleries following one after another there is inevitably one wall – the outside wall – that runs diagonally. The rooms are thus trapezoid in ground plan, and their right-angled ends thrust into the courtyard to different extents, which produces a strangely staggered effect.

Tesar has developed this part of the museum section as a gallery, as a sequence of classical rooms with top-lighting. And as he adapted the light openings in the ceiling precisely to the shape of the room, the lanterns on top are also trapezoid in plan.

In terms of lighting, Tesar varies the top-light system developed by Leo von Klenze for the Alte Pinakothek in Munich, which has scarcely been bettered down to the present day, in a very powerful fashion. The tall, massive lanterns, standing on the top of the gallery section like greenhouses, are closed at the top. They take in daylight through their four glazed walls. Blinds on the outside and fabric curtains that can be drawn on the inside make sure that sunlight cannot penetrate directly into the interior. Thus the light is already diffused in the lantern, and falls evenly, but with intense brightness, into the rooms. And as the walls make a smooth transition to extensive volutes at the top, in other words curve almost imperceptibly towards the lantern shafts, thus produces a wonderfully soft transition between wall and ceiling, without any shadows or dark places.

Tesar had concerned himself intensively with artistic themes and the way in which they can be presented in museums before starting to work as an architect, and thus found a highly subtle solution for the eternal prob-

kantenlos in weit ausholende Vouten übergehen, also sich den Laternenschächten fast unmerklich entgegenwölben, ergibt sich ein wunderbar weicher Übergang zwischen Wand und Decke, der keine Verschattungen, keine dunklen Stellen kennt.

Tesar, der sich, bevor er als Architekt zu arbeiten begann, intensiv mit bildnerischen Themen und mit ihrer Präsentation im musealen Zusammenhang beschäftigt hatte, fand somit in Klosterneuburg eine höchst subtile Lösung für das ewige Problem der Belichtung von Ausstellungsräumen. In vielen der architektonisch einprägsamen Museumsneubauten der letzten dreißig Jahre sind geradezu groteske Experimente gemacht worden, um das Tageslicht einzufangen und zu lenken. Tesar schlägt sich hier bewußt auf die Seite der Tradition, er versteckt die Elemente der Lichtführung nicht in der Dachkonstruktion, er hebt sie absichtsvoll heraus, dehnt die aufgesetzten Laternen fast auf Stockwerkshöhe und macht sie so zu einem selbstbewußt den Außenbau prägenden Architekturmotiv. Und da im Inneren in den Sockeln der Laternenhäuser auch die Schienen für die Zusatzbeleuchtung und die Abluftschlitze versteckt sind, bleiben die sockellos weißen Ausstellungswände von allen störenden Elementen frei; sie stellen sich fast wollüstig in den Dienst der Kunstwerke. Die Galerieräume sind also ideale Schreine für Malerei jeder Größenordnung, was dem Kernbestand der Sammlung entgegenkommt. Doch auch Skulpturen gelangen hier bestens zur Geltung. Für lichtempfindliche Grafik und für Videos aber gibt es eine Black-Box am Anfang des Rundgangs.

Dort, wo die Besucher, aus dem Foyer kommend, die Enfilade der Galerieräume betreten, liegt, noch im Eingangstrakt, die Bibliothek, eine wunderbar intime, zweigeschossige Lesestube. Die Bücherregale an den Wänden, die Arbeitstische und die um den Treppenschacht herumlaufenden Lesepulte sind alle aus einem einzigen, intensiv gemusterten Platanenstamm gefertigt, wodurch der Raum eine herrlich einheitliche Wärme erhält. Der Rest ist Glas: Eine Glaswand gibt den Blick in den ersten Galeriesaal frei, hält somit Kontakt zur Sammlung; eine begehbare, große Glasplatte im Boden der oberen Etage – sie reißt den Blick fast abrupt in die Tiefe – vermittelt in der Bücherklause zwischen oben und unten.

Der über dem Depotgeschoß gelegene Ausstellungstrakt, den die Besucher direkt vom Foyer aus betreten können oder aber am Ende der Galerieflucht erreichen, bildet architektonisch den denkbar größten Gegensatz zu seinem Pendant, dem Galerietrakt. Vom Skulpturenhof aus läßt sich die Formendramaturgie besonders eindrucksvoll studieren: auf der einen Seite die unterschiedlich weit in den Hof sich schiebenden Kuben des Galerietrakts mit den senkrechten Fensterbändern und den hohen leichten Aufbauten der Laternen, die nachts wie Lichtwürfel über dem Ganzen schweben; auf der anderen Seite ein Triumph der Waagerechten, ein langer durchfensterter Riegel, der durch eine schier endlos gedehnte Diagonale, eine langsam ansteigende Rampe, zweigeteilt wird. Über diese Rampe, die auch im Inneren der Halle als plastisches Element raumbildend wirkt, können die Besucher vom Hof aus zur Terrasse hinaufsteigen, die in ganzer Länge oben vor dem Großen Saal entlangläuft. Den Abschluß nach oben bildet das in einer sanften Welle sich aufwölbende Dach des Großen Saals, das als Reflex auf die nahen Weinberghügel gedeutet werden kann.

Vier spannungsvoll kontrastierende horizontale Linien strukturieren also den Ausstellungstrakt auf der Hofseite: die beiden Waagrechten der Stockwerksböden, die Schräge der Rampe und die Welle des Dachs. Als fünftes plastisches Element bestätigt die im Hof liegende lange Rinne aus schwarzem Basalt, in der Wasser fließt, die skulpturalen Qualitäten dieser horizontalen Architekturkomposition.

Die Ausstellungshalle, die, nur durch Querwände unterteilt, den ganzen Trakt durchläuft, erhält ihr Licht und ihr architektonisches Leben durch die beiden Längsseiten. Auf der Hofseite schwingt sich die Rampe als frei plastisches Element langsam nach oben. Unter dem langen Band der Rampe ist der Boden der Ausstellungshalle in ganzer Länge zu den Depots hinab geöffnet. Der Besucher kann dort wie von einer Empore aus hinunterschauen in jenen Bereich, der ihm beim Rundgang sonst verschlossen bleibt; ihn erreicht so eine plötzliche Ahnung von etwas, was in allen anderen Museen peinlich ausgespart bleibt: von dem riesigen Unterleib, der das illustre Leben in den Ausstellungsräumen überhaupt erst möglich macht. Daß der von Tesar als »Raumschnitt« bezeichnete Schacht beiläufig auch noch eine Menge Tageslicht in die sonst hermetisch verschlossene Unterwelt der Depots bringt, ist die nützliche Seite dieses auch bereits rein ästhetisch überzeugenden Eingriffs.

Die Trennwand zwischen Ausstellungshalle und Skulpturenhof ist also höchst ambitioniert ausgebildet. Doch die Wand, die gegenüberliegt, die Außenwand, vermag ihr auf gleichem Niveau zu antworten. Sie öffnet die Halle nicht nach unten in die Depots, sondern nach oben in den Großen Saal. Auf dieser Seite ist eine kleine Rotunde in die Halle eingestellt; sie ist nach oben offen und soll als Konzertmuschel bei Musikveranstaltungen, als Studio für elektroakustische Darbietungen oder raumbezogene Klanginstallationen beide Ausstellungsetagen miteinander verbinden. Durch das Rund ihrer Öffnung bewegt sich auch eine Treppe an der Außenwand nach oben. Auf halber Höhe kann der Besucher auf einem Podest haltmachen und nach innen in die Rotunde oder nach außen durch den querverlaufenden Fensterstreifen auf die Auenlandschaft und die Weinberghügel jenseits der Donau blicken.

Die untere Ausstellungshalle mit ihren Zwischenwänden und dem Gemisch aus natürlichem Seiten- und Kunstlicht hat neben den ästhetisch perfektionierten Oberlichtsälen der Galerie fast Werkstattcharakter; sie eignet sich also für alle möglichen Mischformen der Darbietung, wie sie heute im Ausstellungsbetrieb so beliebt sind, aber auch für kleinformatige Arbeiten. Im Großen Saal darüber aber, der von allen Zwischenwänden freigehalten ist – kommen die großformatigen Bilderserien und die ausladenden Objekte der Sammlung bestens zur Geltung.

Das Motiv der einbeschriebenen Rotunde paraphrasiert eines der Lieblingsmotive Tesars: das Ineinander von rechteckigen und runden Formen. Und noch eine Erinnerung taucht im Großen Saal auf: In die sanft sich aufwölbende und wieder abfallende Decke sind querrechteckige Lichtöffnungen eingelassen; sie dienen, ähnlich wie die runden Lichtkuppeln im Schömer-Haus oder in der evangelischen Kirche sowohl der formalen Belebung als auch der natürlichen Belichtung. Durch die Wölbung bekommt jeder der Lichtschlitze einen anderen Winkel zum Himmel, also auch ein anderes Licht. Und da durch das flache Fensterband in der Außen-

lem of lighting exhibition galleries in Klosterneuburg. There have been some pretty grotesque attempts to capture and direct daylight in many of the architecturally striking new museum buildings of the past thirty years. Tesar puts himself firmly on the side of tradition here. He does not hide the light control elements in the roof structure, he deliberately makes them conspicuous, stretching the lanterns on top of the building almost to the height of a full storey and thus makes them into an architectural motif that makes a self-confident impact on the exterior. And as the tracks for additional lighting and the ventilation slits are also concealed inside, in the bases of the lantern-houses, the white exhibition walls, without skirting-boards, remain free of any disturbing elements; they dedicate themselves almost sensually to serving the works of art. Thus the galleries are ideal shrines for paintings of any size, which suits the core of the collection. But sculptures can also be shown to their best advantage here. For light-sensitive graphic art and videos there is a black box at the start of the sequence of rooms.

At the point where visitors come out of the foyer and start to move through the enfilade of galleries is, still in the entrance section, the library, a wonderfully intimate, two-storey reading room. The bookshelves on the walls, the work-tables and the reading desks arranged around the stairwell are all made from a single plane-tree trunk with a very striking grain, which gives the room a wonderfully uniform warmth. The rest is glass: a glass wall makes it possible to look through to the first gallery space, and thus maintains contact with the collection; a large glass slab, on which visitors can walk, forms the floor of the upper level – it makes one look down almost abruptly – and creates a link between the upper and lower levels of the little library.

The exhibition wing above the storage floor, which visitors can enter directly from the foyer or at the end of the run of galleries, architecturally forms the greatest possible contrast with its opposite number, the gallery wing. The dramatic structure of the forms can be studied particularly impressively from the sculpture courtyard: on one side are the cubes of the gallery wing, pushing out into the courtyard to different extents, with vertical bands of windows and the high, light-weight lantern structures, floating above the whole building like cubes of light at night; on the other side is a triumph of the horizontal, a long bar with windows along its full length, cut in two by a diagonal that seems to go on for ever, a slowly rising ramp. Visitors can use this ramp, which also has the effect of a space-creating, three-dimensional element inside the hall, to go up from the courtyard to the terrace that runs the full length of the Great Hall at the top. The upper conclusion is formed by the gently rising wave of the roof of the Great Hall, which can be interpreted as a response to the nearby hills of the vineyards.

Four horizontal lines, in a tension of contrasts, thus articulate the exhibition wing on the courtyard side: the two horizontals of the floors of the storeys, the diagonal of the ramp and the wave of the roof. As a fifth three-dimensional element, the long black basalt rill in which water flows confirms the sculptural qualities of this horizontal architectural composition.

The exhibition hall is divided only by transverse walls, and runs the full length of the section. It gains its light and architectural life from the two long sides. On the courtyard side the ramps slowly climbs upwards as a free sculptural element. Under the long band of the ramp, the floor of the exhibition hall opens down to the stores along its full length. Visitors can look down from there as from a gallery at this area, which would normally be closed to them as they walk round; they are thus suddenly given an idea of something that is embarrassingly omitted in all other museums: the gigantic underbody without which the illustrious life in the exhibition rooms would not be possible at all. The shaft that Tesar calls a »spatial section« also happens to provide the otherwise closed underworld of the stores with quite a lot of light, which is the practical side of this intervention that is already convincing on purely aesthetic grounds.

So the dividing wall between the sculpture courtyard and the exhibition hall is structured very ambitiously. But the wall opposite, the outside wall, is able to respond to it on the same level. It does not open down to the space to the stores below, but upwards into the Great Hall. On this side a small rotunda is inserted into the space; it is open at the top, and is intended to link the two exhibition floors, as a concert shell at musical events, as a studio for electronic sound presentations or space-related sound installations. A flight of steps also moves upwards on the outside wall, through the round aperture. Visitors can stop on a landing half-way up and look inwards into the rotunda and outwards through the transverse strips of windows at the meadows and the hilly vineyards on the other side of the Danube.

The lower exhibition hall with its intermediate walls and a mixture of natural side-lighting and artificial light is almost workshop-like in contrast with the aesthetically perfected top-lit rooms in the gallery; it is thus suitable for all possible mixed forms of presentation of the kind that are so popular in the world of exhibitions today, but also for smaller-format works. But series of large-format pictures and the more sizeable object in the collection show to their best effect in the Great Hall above.

The motive of the inscribed rotunda is a paraphrase of one of Tesar's favourite themes: linking rectangular and circular forms. And another memory crops up in the Great Hall: transverse-rectangular light openings are let into the ceiling, which curves gently upwards and then dips down again; rather like the round light-domes in the Schömer-Haus or in the Protestant church they serve to enliven the form, but also as a source of natural light. The curve means that each of the light slits is at a different angle to the sky, and thus admits a different kind of light. And thus the Great Hall, unlike the galleries, which have totally calmed lighting, has different light situations as the shallow band of windows in the outside wall and the large French windows at the end of the inside wall admit additional light.

If visitors leave the Great Hall and move on to the long terrace, which is also used by the café, they can make an impressive comparison of the three sections surrounding the courtyard and their contrasting building forms. And from up here, standing opposite the lanterns on the gallery section, there is also a particularly beautiful view to the west of the foothills of the Vienna Woods. But to the north is the town of Klosterneuburg with the massive Chorherrenstift complex directly in view from the little round outlook cockpit; it gives visitors at least an idea of the forward-thrusting tip of the triangle of the building, of the building's con-

wand und durch die großen Fenstertüren an den Enden der Innenwand zusätzlich Licht einfällt, ergeben sich, ganz im Gegensatz zu den in der Beleuchtung völlig beruhigten Galerieräumen, im Großen Saal verschiedene Lichtsituationen, die den Raum atmosphärisch aufteilen und beleben.

Tritt man aus dem Saal hinaus auf die lange Terrasse, die auch vom Café genutzt wird, kann man nicht nur die drei den Hof rahmenden Trakte in ihren gegensätzlichen Bauformen eindrucksvoll miteinander vergleichen, es tut sich von hier oben, wo man den Laternen des Galerietrakts gegenübersteht, auch ein besonders schöner Blick nach Westen auf die Ausläufer des Wienerwalds auf. Im Norden aber liegt die Stadt Klosterneuburg mit dem gewaltigen Massiv des Stifts direkt im Blickfeld der kleinen runden Aussichtskanzel; sie gibt dem Besucher wenigstens eine Ahnung von der vorgeschobenen Spitze des Gebäudedreiecks, von der architektonisch höchst eigenwillig ausgeprägten Abschlußgeste des Hauses in Richtung Stadt.

Wie so oft in seinen Bauten, etwa am Vordach des Schömer-Hauses, läßt Tesar eine der Außenlinien über das geometrische Grundgerüst hinauslaufen und in einem kurvigen Zipfel, einem gebauten Schnörkel enden. Hier, beim Museum, münden die beiden nach Norden zielenden geraden Außenwände jeweils in eine Kurve: Die westliche Wand endet in einem kleinen runden Erker, der im oberen Ausstellungsgeschoß als Terrasse nutzbar ist; die östliche Wand läuft mit einem schmalen Gebäudestreifen noch ein ganzes Stück weiter nach Norden, schwenkt dann in mehreren Brüchen nach innen und bildet so einen quasi geschuppten, spitz endenden Gebäudezipfel, der sich im Charakter deutlich von der geschlossenen Masse des Museumsbaus unterscheidet. Er umschreibt mit seiner einwärts gedrehten Geste eine Art Binnenhof, einen angedeuteten, magisch aufgeladenen Raum, den der Architekt als Rosengarten gestaltet und mit einer seiner skulpturalen Arbeiten besetzt hat.

Dieser kapriziöse Tesar-Schnörkel ist formal wie inhaltlich deutlich vom Dreieck der übrigen Trakte abgesetzt. Man könnte ihn als die architektonische Kür nach Absolvierung der Pflicht einstufen. Das Hauptgeschoß endet an der Nordspitze in einem großzügigen Konferenzraum. Ihm kommen die beiden Architekturausleger zugute. In den mit schmalen Fensterschlitzen versehenen Runderker ist eine Sitznische hineinmodelliert, die zu entspanntem Plaudern einlädt. Der nach Norden ausschreitende, am Ende schneckenartig gewendelte Anbau aber bewährt sich als angenehm heller Besprechungsraum. Seine geknickte Spitze ist an den Knickstellen mit schmalen senkrechten Fensterstreifen versehen, die zwangsläufig jeweils in eine andere Richtung zielen und so den kleinen Wurmfortsatz zu einer einprägsamen, aller Nützlichkeit enthobenen, vom Licht und von der Aussicht bestimmten Raumfigur machen. Im Stockwerk darüber, in der Höhe des Großen Saals, ist über dem Konferenzraum ein privates Arbeitszimmer für Karlheinz Essl eingerichtet. Und wie beim Erker dient auch hier der ausscherende Annex als Terrasse. Der Stifter kann hier also mit seinen Gästen und Künstlerfreunden auf eine weit vorgestreckte, dem Museumsbetrieb entzogene Kanzel hinaustreten und den schönen Rundumblick auf die Landschaft und die Stadt genießen.

Wäre Essl vom österreichischen Staat in das neue Museumsquartier in den Wiener Hofstallungen eingeladen worden, hätte er seine Sammlung mit den kaiserlichen Hinterlassenschaften, mit den berühmten Museen am Ring messen können. In Klosterneuburg kann er nun im eigenen Haus selbstbewußt dem ähnlich großartigen Baukomplex des Chorherrenstifts gegenübertreten. Hier fehlen zwar die musealen Vergleichsmaßstäbe, die den Rang seiner Sammlung bestätigen würden, doch der Soloauftritt im architektonisch eigenwilligen, mit allen museologischen Finessen bestückten Baukomplex wirkt noch um einiges ausdrucksvoller als die Einbindung in die staatlichen Sammlungen.

Der Trotz, der mit im Spiel gewesen sein dürfte, als die Essls sich von der Wiener Vision verabschiedeten und zu einem eigenen Museumsbau entschlossen, er hat in der nach außen fast abweisenden Klosterneuburger Museumsarchitektur seine symbolische Ausformung gefunden. Daß die drei exponierten Eckpunkte des Stiftungsbollwerks wie die Türme einer Burg jeweils für ein anderes Mitglied der Familie bestimmt sind, das ist nicht nur ein sichtbares Zeichen für das gewachsene Selbstbewußtsein der Stifter, es zeigt auch, wie direkt Agnes und Karlheinz Essl sowie ihr komponierender Sohn das künstlerische Leben in der Stiftung mitbestimmen wollen, wie entschieden sie die Spielwiese des Hauses als eines ihrer Arbeitsfelder betrachten.

Die drei familiären Arbeitsräume über dem Kulturzentrum lassen am privaten Charakter der Stiftung also keinen Zweifel aufkommen. Doch die Funktionen des Museums werden durch das ausgespannte Kräftenetz nirgendwo eingeschränkt. Der Besucher spürt von den organisatorischen Hintergründen wenig, er erlebt die Präsentation der Sammlung als reinen Glücksfall, die Architektur aber als ein ästhetisches Abenteuer, als Erfüllung mancher Wünsche, die von anderen neuen Museumsbauten geweckt, aber nicht erfüllt wurden.

Heinz Tesar hat die künstlerischen Freiheiten, die ihm der Bauherr einräumte, genutzt und intensiv nach Lösungen für jene Probleme gesucht, die bei öffentlichen Museumsbauten oft nur angedacht werden. So wird sein Haus für die Sammlung Essl nicht nur in seinem eigenen Œuvre einen prominenten Platz einnehmen, es wird auch in der keineswegs langweiligen Geschichte des neueren Museumsbaus eine bedeutende Rolle spielen.

Vor allem mit seinen vielfältigen Methoden der Lichtzufuhr und seinen wechselnden Raumfiguren für die Auftrittsrituale der zeitgenössischen Kunst hat Tesar Maßstäbe gesetzt. Seine ausgeklügelte Variante der klassischen Oberlichtlaterne und sein leicht zu bedienendes Aufbewahrungssystem für Bilder sollten zum Lernprogramm aller Hochschulen gehören. Insgesamt ist es aber wohl das zwanglose und doch höchst sinnfällige In- und Nebeneinander der verschiedenen Museumsfunktionen, das den Reiz der kompakten Raumkomposition in Klosterneuburg ausmacht.

Tesars Museumsbau schafft etwas, was eigentlich ein Widerspruch ist: Er stellt sich ganz in den Dienst der ausgestellten Kunstwerke und profiliert sich gerade mit dieser Besonderheit als architektonisches Individuum, als autonomes Bau-Kunstwerk. Mit seiner enigmatischen Erscheinung läßt er etwas von jenem Geheimnis ahnen, das den Künsten eigentlich immer zu eigen sein sollte, das in den letzten Jahrzehnten aber – auch durch allzu aufgeregte Museumsarchitekturen – oft verspielt worden ist.

cluding gesture towards the town, which bears a most unconventional stamp in architectural terms.

Tesar, as he so often does in his buildings, in the canopy of the Schömer-Haus, for example, allows one of the outside lines to run out of the basic geometrical framework and end in a curved tip, a built flourish. Here, in the museum, the two north-pointing, straight walls each end in a curve: the west wall in a little rounded bay that can be used as a terrace on the upper exhibition floor; the east wall continues quite a lot further north in the form of a narrow strip of building, then swings inwards in several breaks and thus forms a more or less scaled tip for the building ending in a point, which is clearly different in character from the closed mass of the museum building. Its inward-turning gesture surrounds a kind of inner courtyard, an indicated, magically charged space that the architect has designed as a rose garden and has placed one of his sculptures in it.

This capricious flourish by Tesar is clearly set apart from the triangle of the other sections in terms of both form and content. It could be categorized as a piece of architectural treatment in a spa after one's duty has been done. The main floor ends in a generously sized conference room at its northern tip. It benefits from both the architectural outriggers. Modelled into the round bay, which has narrow window slits, is a niche for sitting that invites visitors to relax and chat. But the extension to the building that moves out towards the north, spiralling like a snail at the end, holds its own as a pleasantly light meeting-room. Its indented tip has narrow vertical window-strips at each kink, which inevitably all point in different directions and thus make the little worm-like continuation into a memorable spatial figure, not serving any practical purpose and defined by light and the view. On the upper floor, at the level of the Great Hall, Karlheinz Essl has his own study above the conference room. And as in the case of the bay, the annexe that breaks out at this point also serves as a terrace. The man who gave all this to the town can thus step out with this guests and artist friends on to a cockpit that thrusts well forward and is away from the business of the museum, and enjoy the beautiful panoramic view of the countryside and the town.

If Essl had been invited by the Austrian state into the new museum quarter in the court stables in Vienna he would have been able to measure his collection against the legacy of the empire, the famous museums on the Ring. In Klosterneuburg he can stand in his own building and confidently face the similarly magnificent complex of buildings that make up the Chorherrenstift. Certainly there are no comparisons here in the form of museums to confirm the status of his collection, but the solo appearance in a building complex that is architecturally unconventional and fitted out with every possible item of museum finesse seems considerably more impressive that being tied in with the state collections.

The defiance that must have come into play when the Essls said goodbye to the Vienna vision and decided to build their own museum has found symbolic form in the architecture of the Klosterneuburg museum, which is almost forbidding from the outside. The fact that the three exposed corner points of the foundation's bastion, like the towers of a castle, are each intended for a different member of the family is not just a visible sign of the founder's mature self-confidence.

It also shows that Agnes and Karlheinz Essl and their composer son intend to keep to shape the artistic life of the foundation, and how definitely they see the playground offered by the building as a field in which they want to work.

And so the three workrooms for the members of the family above the culture centre leave no doubt about the private character of the foundation. But the functions of the museum are not restricted at any point by the outstretched network of forces. Visitors have little sense of the organization going on in the background, they experience the presentation of the collection as a happy chance, but the architecture as an aesthetic adventure, as the fulfilment of many a desire that has been awoken by other new museum buildings, but not satisfied.

Heinz Tesar has made full use of the artistic liberties allowed him by his client, and sought intensively for solutions that for all the problems that are often only half considered in public museum buildings. Thus his building for the Essl Collection will not only occupy a prominent place in his own œuvre, it will also play an important part in the by no means boring story of recent museum architecture.

Tesar has set standards above all with his many methods for providing light and his changing spatial configurations for the appearance rituals of contemporary art. His ingenious variation on the classical toplight lantern and his easy-to-use method for storing pictures should be part of the course at all institutes of higher education. But overall it is probably the free-and-easy and yet highly intelligent linking and juxtaposition of the various museum functions that explain the charm of this compact spatial composition in Klosterneuburg.

Tesar's museum building creates something that is actually a contradiction: it puts itself entirely at the service of the works of art exhibited, and establishes itself as an architectural individual, as a built work of art in its own right with precisely this special feature. Its enigmatic appearance gives some idea of the mystery that should always be part of the arts, but that has often been squandered in recent decades by some unduly agitated museum architecture.

1. Perspekive der Gesamtsituation.
2. Lageplan.

1. Perspective view of the general situation.
2. Site plan.

S. 18, 19
3–6. Grundrisse (Ebenen 0/1, 2/3, 4/5) und Dachaufsicht).

p. 18, 19
3–6. Floor plans (levels 0/1, 2/3, 4/5) and top view.

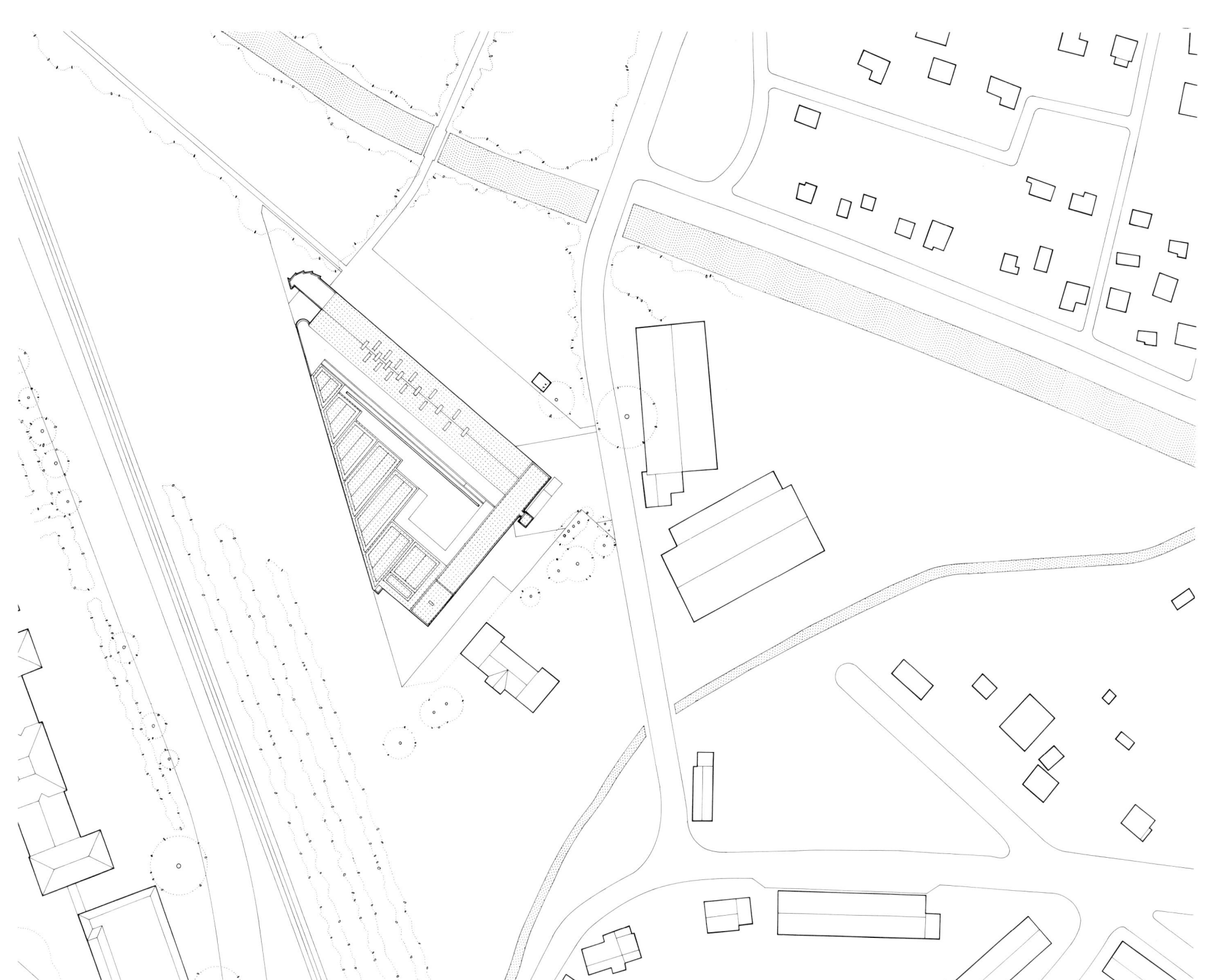

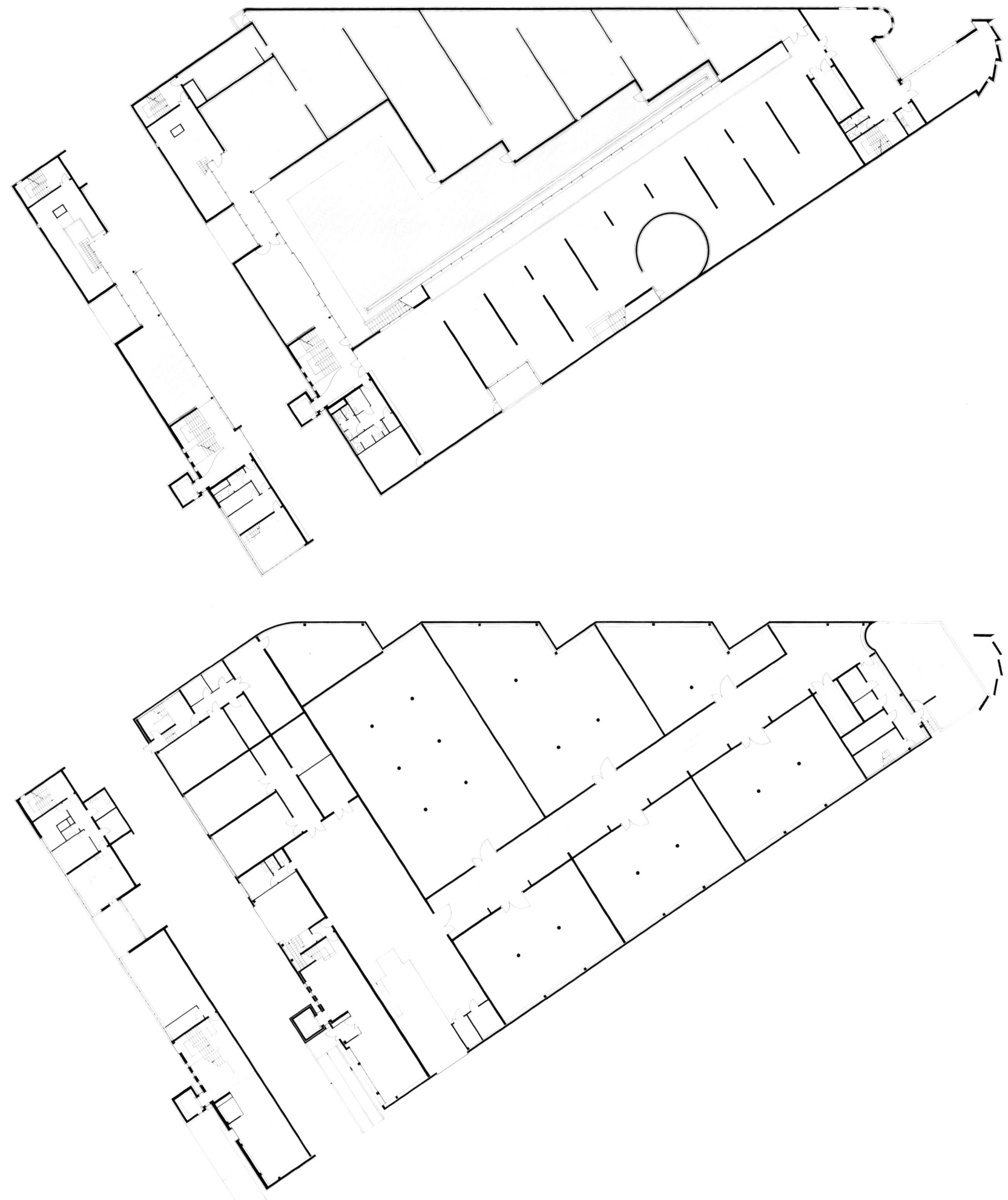

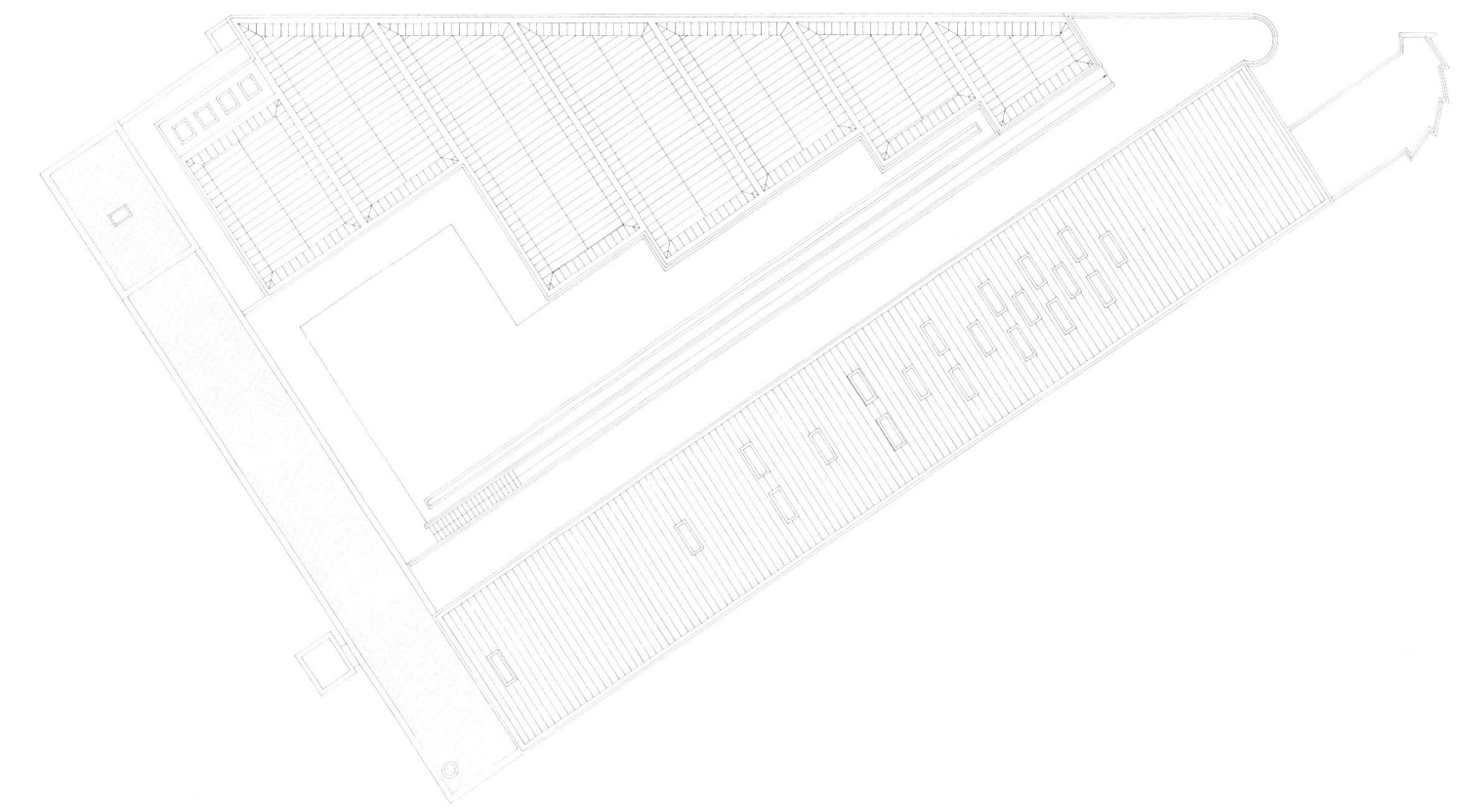

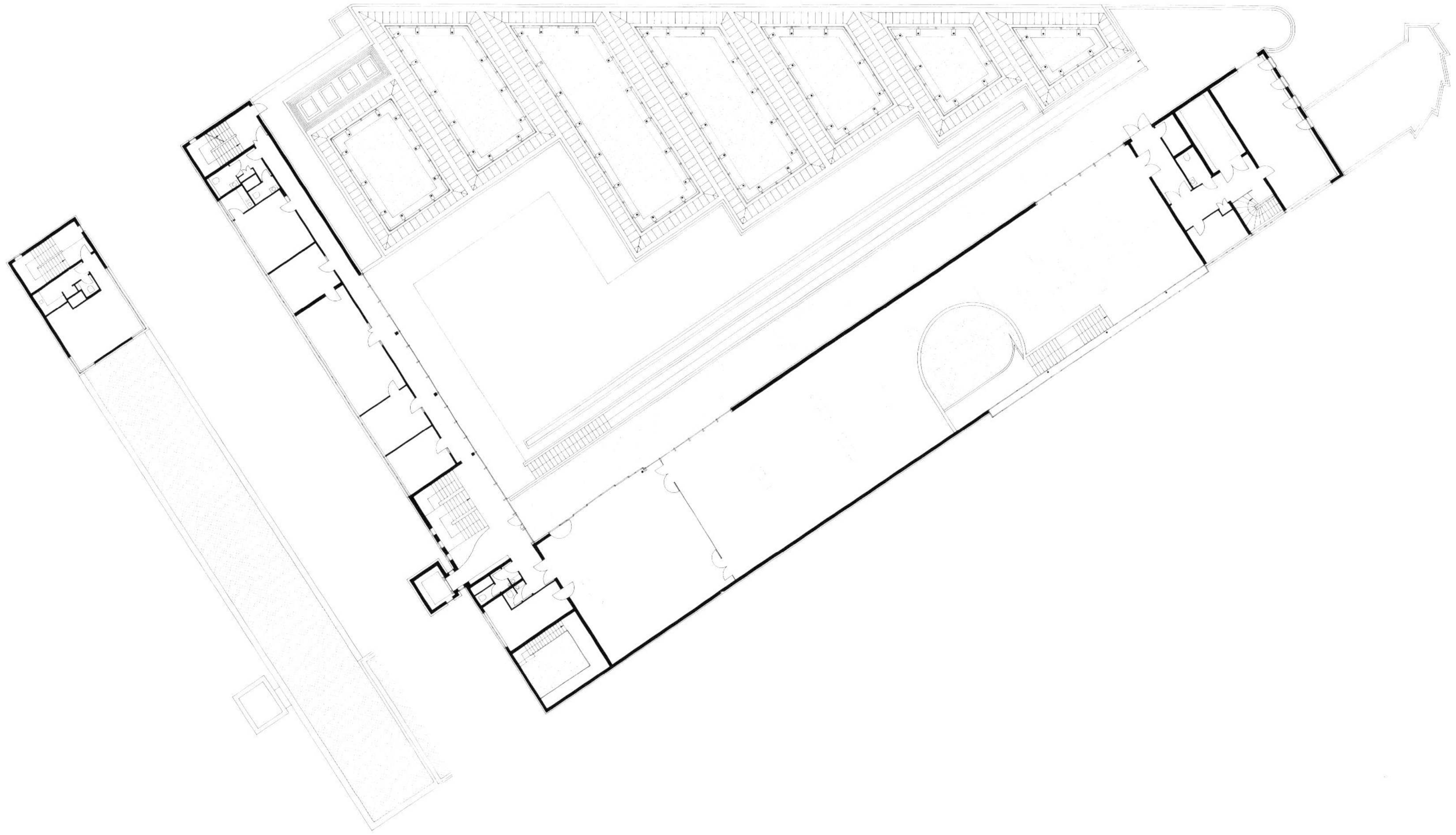

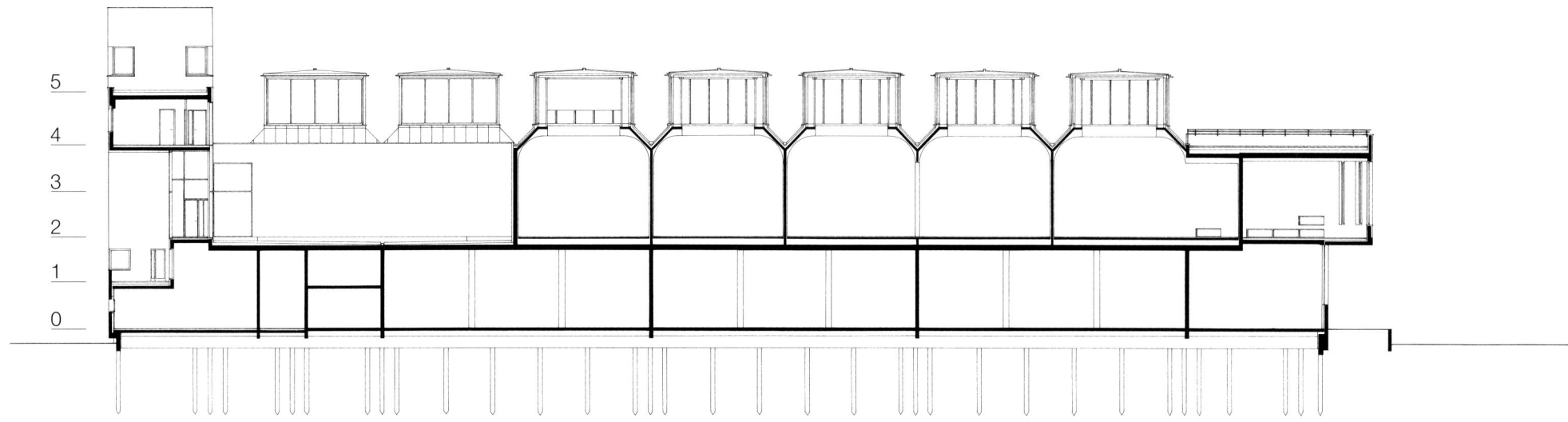

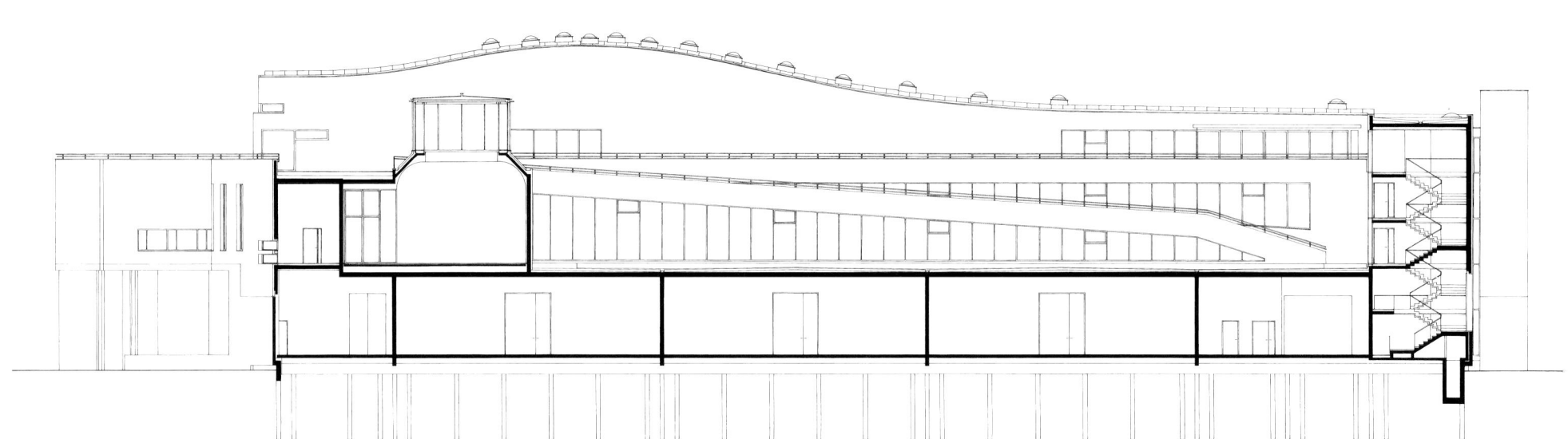

7–12. Schnitte und Aufrisse.

7–12. Sections and elevations.

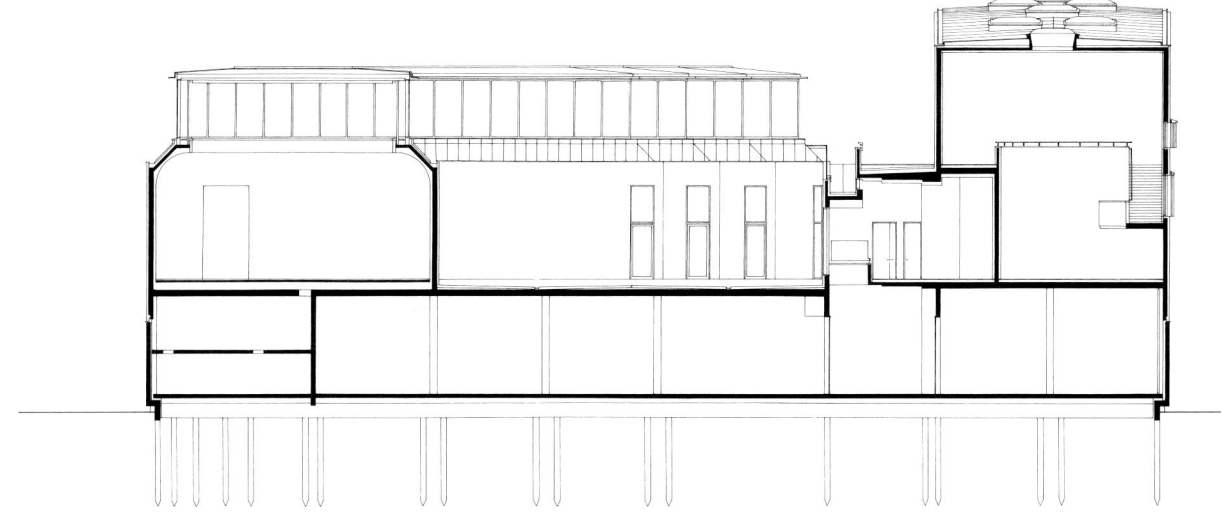

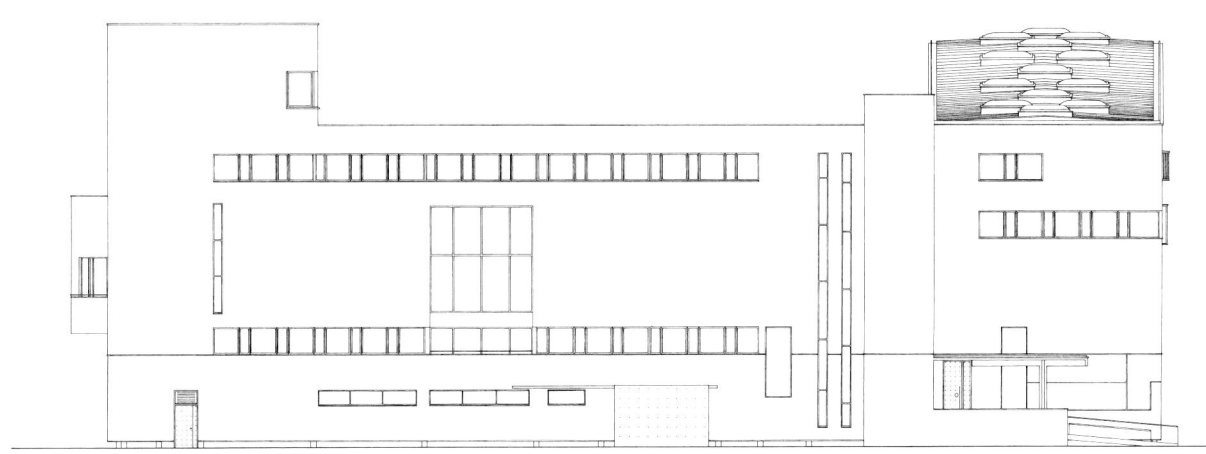

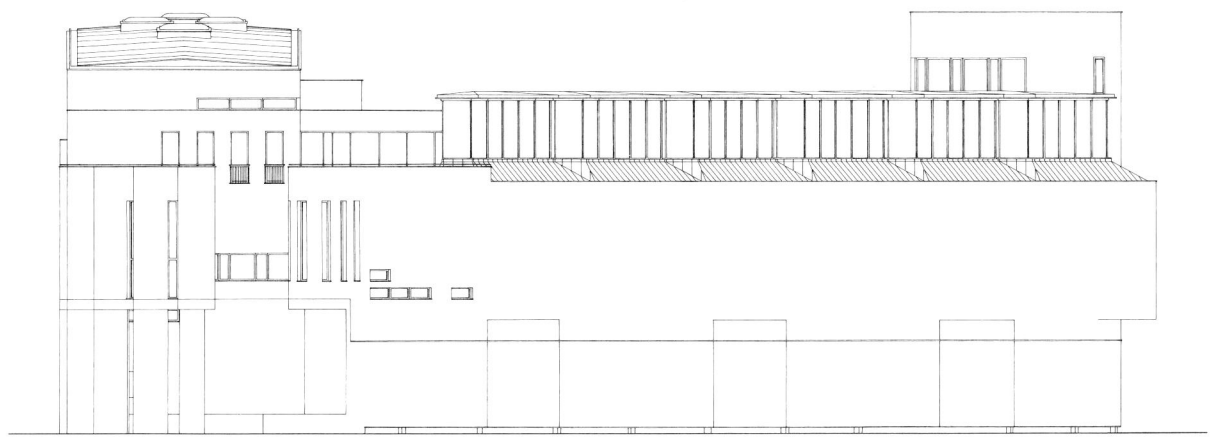

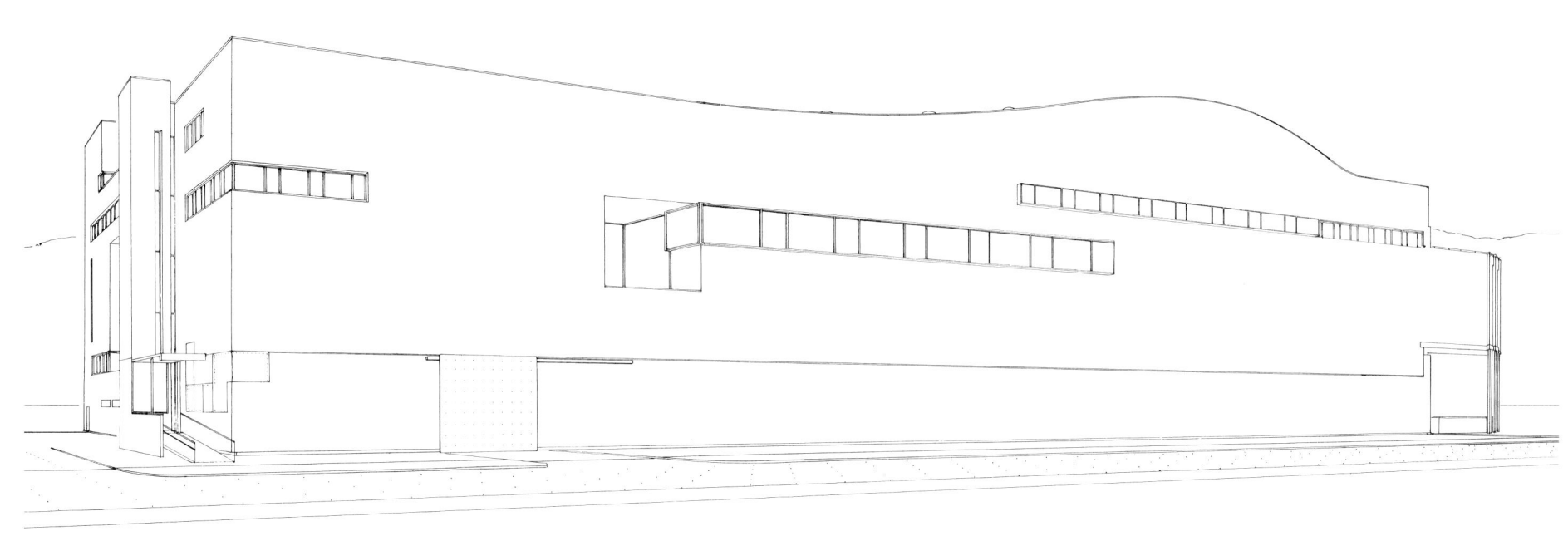

13, 14. Perspektiven.

13, 14. Perspective views.

S. 24/25
1. Gesamtansicht von Nordwesten. Im Hintergrund die Stadt Wien mit den Türmen der Donau City.

p. 24/25
1. General view from the northwest. In the background the city of Vienna with the towers of the Donau City.

2. Gesamtansicht von Nordwesten.
3. Gesamtansicht von Süden.
4. Gesamtansicht von Südwesten.

2. General view from the northwest.
3. General view from the south.
4. General view from the southwest.

S. 28/29
5. Gesamtansicht von Westen.

p. 28/29
5. General view from the west.

6. Gesamtansicht von Osten mit Hauptzugang.
7. Gesamtansicht von Norden.

6. General view from the east with main entrance.
7. General view from the north.

S. 32, 33
8. Detailansicht von Osten.
9. Detailansicht von Norden.

p. 32, 33
8. Detailed view from the east.
9. Detailed view from the north.

S. 34, 35
10, 11. Detailansichten der nördlichen Spitze des Gebäudes.

p. 34, 35
10, 11. Detailed views of the north corner of the building.

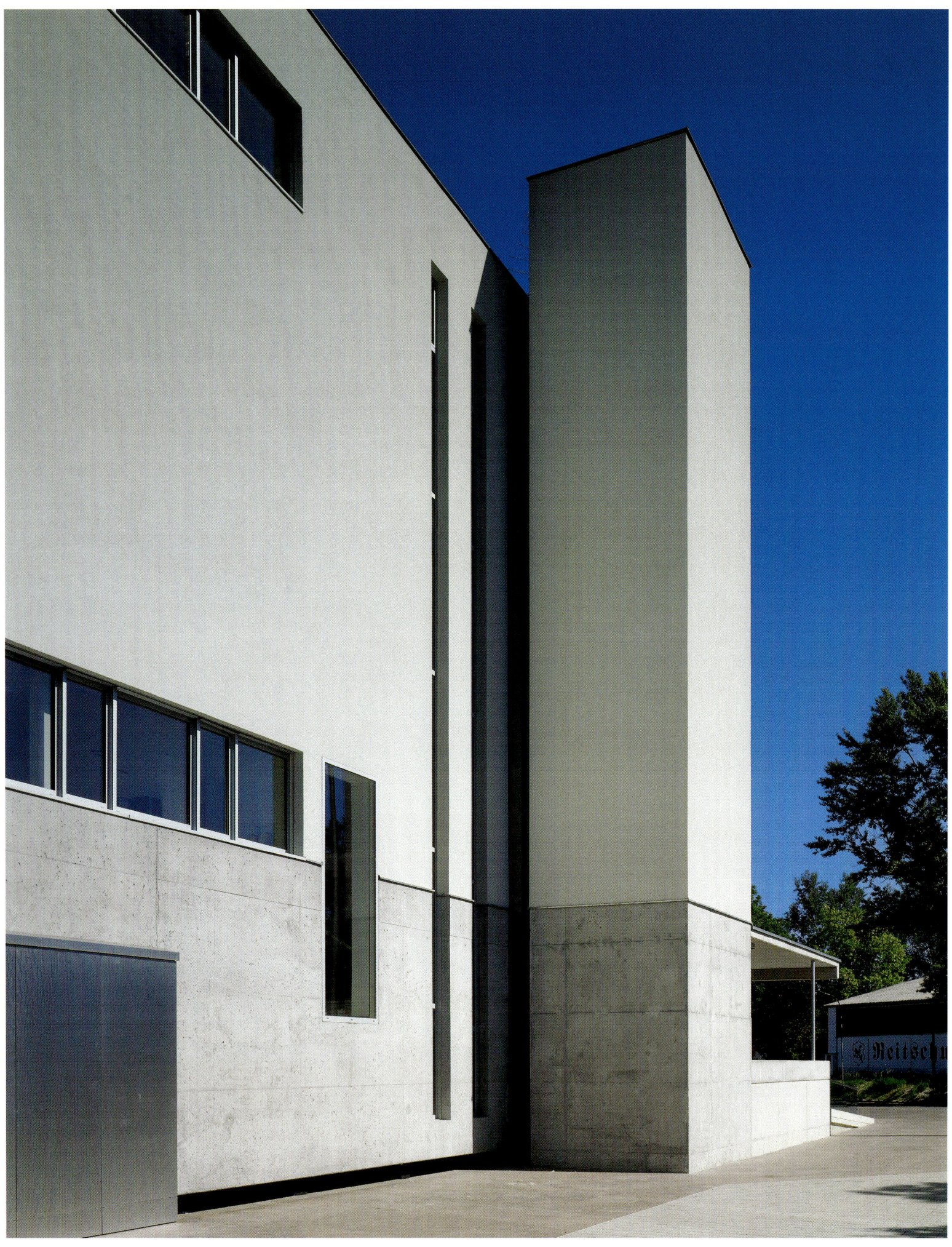

S. 36, 37
12, 13. Detailansichten der östlichen Spitze des Gebäudes mit Hauptzugang.

p. 36, 37
12, 13. Detailed views of the east corner of the building with main entrance.

14, 15. Das Haupttreppenhaus.

14, 15. The main staircase.

16. Der Innenhof. Links der Galerietrakt, rechts der Ausstellungstrakt.
17, 18. Detailansichten der Laternen auf dem Galerietrakt.

16. The courtyard. The gallery wing to the left, the exhibition wing to the right.
17, 18. Detailed views of the lanterns on the gallery wing.

S. 42, 43
19. Der Galerietrakt mit Gemälden von Karel Appel, Georg Baselitz und Otto Zitko.
20. Der Galerietrakt mit Gemälden von Emilio Vedova und Asger Jorn.

p. 42, 43
19. The gallery wing with paintings by Karel Appel, Georg Baselitz and Otto Zitko.
20. The gallery wing with paintings by Emilio Vedova and Asger Jorn.

21. Der Galerietrakt mit Gemälden von Per Kirkeby, Max Weiler und Asger Jorn.
22. Der Galerietrakt mit Gemälden von Georg Baselitz, Karel Appel und Per Kirkeby.

21. The gallery wing with paintings by Per Kirkeby, Max Weiler and Asger Jorn.
22. The gallery wing with paintings by Georg Baselitz, Karel Appel and Per Kirkeby.

23. Der Galerietrakt mit Gemälden von Maria Lassnig, Peter Kogler, Pierre Soulages sowie Skulpturen von Marc Quinn und Fritz Wotruba.
24. Der Galerietrakt mit Gemälden von Pierre Soulages und Emilio Vedova sowie einer Skulptur von Fritz Wotruba.

23. The gallery wing with paintings by Maria Lassnig, Peter Kogler, Pierre Soulages and skulptures by Marc Quinn and Fritz Wotruba.
24. The gallery wing with paintings by Pierre Soulages and Emilio Vedova and a sculpture by Fritz Wotruba.

25, 26. Das untere Geschoß des Ausstellungstraktes mit Gemälden von Wolfgang Hollegha, Dieter Roth, Hans Staudacher und Martin Kippenberger.

25, 26. The lower floor of the exhibition wing with paintings by Wolfgang Hollegha, Dieter Roth, Hans Staudacher and Martin Kippenberger.

27. Das untere Geschoß des Ausstellungstraktes mit Skulpturen von Mimmo Palladino und Franz West.
28. Die über zwei Geschosse reichende »Rotunde« im Ausstellungstrakt.

27. The lower floor of the exhibition wing with sculptures by Mimmo Palladino and Franz West.
28. The two-storey »rotunda« in the exhibition wing.

S. 52/53
29. Der Große Saal im oberen Geschoß des Ausstellungstraktes mit Gemälden von Markus Lüpertz und Gilbert & George sowie Skulpturen von Nam June Paik, Jannis Kounellis und Markus Lüpertz.

p. 52/53
29. The Great Hall on the upper floor of the exhibition wing with paintings by Markus Lüpertz and Gilbert & George and sculptures by Nam June Paik, Jannis Kounellis and Markus Lüpertz.

30, 31. Der Große Saal mit Gemälden von Markus Lüpertz und Gilbert & George sowie einer Skulptur von Markus Lüpertz.
30, 31. The Great Hall with a painting by Markus Lüpertz and Gilbert & George and a sculpture by Markus Lüpertz.

32, 33. Das Depot.

32, 33. The storage area.

S. 58/59
34. Gesamtansicht von Südwesten bei Nacht.

p. 58/59
34. General view from the southwest at night.

**Sammung Essl
Klosterneuburg
An der Donau-Au 1**

Bauherr/BauphysikClients
Fritz Schömer GmbH, Klosterneuburg

Architekt/Architect
Heinz Tesar, Wien/Vienna
Projektleitung/Project management: Susanne Veit
Mitarbeiter/Collaborators: Oliver Aschenbrenner,
Ruedi Bühlmann, Urs Geiger, Kathrin Grumböck,
Johann Osterrieder, Silvia Prager, Franz Steinberger,
Marc Tesar

Projektsteuerung/Project management
Pörner + Partner, Wien/Vienna

Statik/Statics
Christian Aste, Innsbruck

Haustechnik/Mechanical engineering
Euconsult GmbH, Wien/Vienna

Lichtplanung/Lighting design
Charles Keller Design AG, St. Gallen

Klimatechnik/Air-conditioning
PME Technisches Büro für Klimatechnik GmbH,
Ollern, Niederösterreich

Bauphysik/Structural physics
Walter Prause, Wien/Vienna

Bauunternehmen/Main contractor
Ing. E. Auböck GmbH, Enns, Oberösterreich

Möblierung/Furnishing
Vitra GmbH, Wien/Vienna
Ing. Gerhard Graschopf GmbH, Gresten, Niederösterreich